Table of Contents

Foreword

Whenever my house starts to smell deliciously divine around two in the afternoon, I think of Stacy Myers. I find myself wishing we could sit down at the same table and chat while eating that dinner, because man – we'd talk halfway to forever (and then some).

It's on those days that I reach around and pat myself on the back for being smart enough to use a slow cooker meal, and almost 100% of the recipes I've been relying on for those busy days since our real food transition come from Stacy's first slow cooker cookbook, _Crock On!_

Maybe it's because Stacy clearly has a thing for cumin and chili powder, or because she knows how to do things quickly without fluff or extra dishes, or because it's fun to laugh while reading a recipe, but every single one of her dishes has been well-loved by my whole family and many are in the regular rotation at our house.

The busier our family gets, the more I run into problem dinnertimes. Problems because no matter how well I think I planned the meal for the day's schedule, either I don't start early enough, I get interrupted, or I mis-time the total length of food preparation. And that's a problem – I hate the feeling of saying to my son, "Quick, you have 7-and-a-half minutes to eat before we have to leave for soccer!"

So I can't tell you how excited I am about a new crock pot collection from Stacy. My family needs a less-stressed mama, and the laughter and easy prep are going to do that for us. Plus, I like thinking about Stacy at 2 p.m. I think she probably likes it too...join me, and dive in to these recipes to save your sanity and save your supper.

~Katie

Kitchen Stewardship
www.kitchenstewardship.com

I didn't know I would write a second slow cooker cookbook. I thought one would be my thang…but y'all went hog wild and pig crazy over the first one, so I decided a sequel was in order. ;-)

I do so love my crock. I love ~~burning~~ creating new recipes in it and passing them along to you. I make all the mistakes so you don't have too. You can't ask for much more than that. And if you can, I don't want to hear about it. Ha!

This cookbook is called **Keep Crockin': A Poorganic Slow Cooker Cookbook**. Why is that? Well, because we're not an organic family. We enjoy whole, REAL foods. But for the most part, we don't buy organic foods. We cannot afford to do so. We do, however, afford to buy fresh produce and minimally processed foods.

This cookbook is for:

- The person who is super busy and needs something for dinner, but can't find the time at 5pm to cook.
- The person who likes to eat, but burns stuff on the stove and in the oven. *Cough*
- The person who wants to eat crock pot meals, but doesn't want all the cream-of-junk soups.
- The person who likes to read cookbooks for fun because of the pretty pictures.
- You. You. You.

In the spirit of my previous cookbook, I will offer that this one is also semi-whole foods. I have to cover my behind and say "semi," lest I get more emails about how I'm scamming people because canned tomatoes are actually processed foods.

Let me be clear – "processed" for me, means *already prepared food in a can, box, or bag*. Think Rice-A-Roni, Cream-of-Everything, or Stove-Top Stuffing My Belly. So, sit back, relax and enjoy this cookbook… then get off your fanny and make dinner. Feast on food that is GOOD FOR YOU. It's a beautiful thing.

As with any other cookbook, I encourage you to share your favorite recipe(s) with friends. However, I've worked for over a year on this beautiful creation and I expect you will not give away the entire book to someone, but will instead encourage them to purchase their own copy at _keepcrockin.com_.

One last thought. It is copyright infringement (and bad SEO practice) to post an entire recipe verbatim on a website. If you decide to post a recipe from this book, it is imperative that you write your own directions and credit me for the recipe itself. If you have questions about the appropriate use of recipes from this book on your website, please _contact me_.

Stacy

Ingredients & Substitutions

Let's talk ingredients. I mostly use easy-to-find ingredients for my recipes. That being said, you might need to know that I buy a lot of food online from places like Amazon, Vitacost, and Tropical Traditions.

Ingredients you will find in my recipes:

- Coconut flour
- Almond Flour
- Glucomannan (a thickener, but you can also use arrowroot/cornstarch)
- Truvia
- Stevia

If an ingredient I have used can be substituted with something else, I will note it in the ingredients or in the notes below.

Please feel free to play around with the types of flours and sweeteners, but keep in mind that I have tested these recipes and know they work as is…and you run the risk of having the recipe not turn out if you try something different. However, you also run the risk of having it be kick-butt awesome!

With Truvia, I do not buy the stuff in the store. It has a bunch of added fillers that I don't care to spend my money on. So, I make _homemade Truvia_ instead…and we like it better. Much cheaper too – bet you're not surprised, coming from me.

Why do I use alternative sweeteners and "weird" flours? Well, I enjoy cooking with all sorts of ingredients!

Since our family is mostly sugar-free, you'll notice that most of my recipes call for stevia or xylitol. I've tried to make this easier on you by also giving the sugar equivalent. I know that I also have some candida friends who read my cookbooks, so keep in mind that you can sub out sugar in equal parts with xylitol.

So, there's my take on that. And as always, you can _holler at me_ with questions any time.

The Equipment

Let's talk crocks for just a minute. What kind of crock should you use? I'll tell you – one that works. Ha, ha! Once, I put dinner in the crock but it was broken and I didn't know...I came back later and dinner was still cold. Oops. We held a memorial service for the crock, not dinner. *Sniff, sniff*

But really, I note in the recipes what size crock is best for that particular recipe. If you deviate too much from my guidelines on crock size, you might get in trouble. A smaller crock will cook better with small amounts. If you put that same small amount in a large crock, your meal will be done more quickly and you also run the risk of burning dinner. Or so I hear from OTHER PEOPLE. *Cough*

Try to stick within 1 quart of the size I list. That should cover you.

I use the Hamilton Beach Nesting Set in the sizes 2, 4, and 6 quart. I also have a Hamilton Beach 5 quart crock...and I'm thinking about investing in a 3 quart – still pondering. If you want to buy the same crocks I use, visit the _Keep Crockin' Resource Page_.

I like the Hamilton Beach Nesting Set best because it takes up way less space than having 3 separate sizes. This is actually my second set, as I worked the other one to death like a workhorse. They do not cook too hot and my food turns out great every time. I am a fan of the Hamilton Beach brand.

And no, I'm not an affiliate with Hamilton Beach – but I should be, as much as I advertise for them. ;-)

Hamilton Beach Nesting Set

Hamilton Beach 5 Quart

Breakfasts

Apple Breakfast Bread Pudding

I love breakfast. It's my favorite meal of the day. Pair it with one of my favorite appliances, and I get downright giddy. ...And apples. I LOVE APPLES. Apples + Breakfast + Crock Pot = Stacy's Happy Place.

INGREDIENTS:

- 6 cups cubed Sourdough bread
- 1 cup unsweetened applesauce
- 3 egg whites (½ cup)
- 2 teaspoons vanilla
- ½ cup sugar/xylitol/sucanat
- 1 cup milk (whole or almond)
- 1 teaspoon cinnamon
- 1 apple, cored and chopped
- Cinnamon
- Maple syrup for serving

DIRECTIONS:

1. Place cubed bread in the bottom of a greased crock (5 quart).
2. Sprinkle with apple pieces.
3. In a mixing bowl, combine applesauce, egg whites, vanilla, milk, sugar, and cinnamon.
4. Pour over bread cubes. Press down lightly to coat all pieces.
5. Sprinkle top with cinnamon.
6. Cover and cook on HIGH for 1½-2 hours or until center is set.
7. Serve hot with maple syrup.

Yield: 6 servings

Notes:
- I like to get up early, so I prep all of this the night before (including the apple that I chop and place in a container of water) and then put it together first thing in the morning. Two hours later, breakfast is ready! This is a great weekend breakfast.
- I don't normally use crock liners, but I do like a liner for this recipe. I still grease the liner with my Misto. You can find more details on the Misto on the _Keep Crockin' Reference Page_.

This apple bread pudding is creamy and comforting. Perfect for breakfast or a cold winter night. It warms my belly.
++Mark: the husband behind Sweet Kisses and Dirty Dishes

Breakfast

Breakfast Enchiladas

Breakfast is my favorite meal of the day. It's my favorite meal to plan, but more importantly it's my favorite meal to EAT. Get. In. My. Belly. I don't understand people who say, "Well, I just don't like breakfast." WHAT'S THE MATTER WITH YOU?! Seek professional counseling. And then make this. You'll stop saying that silly stuff. Everyone loves bacon.

INGREDIENTS:

- 18 slices deli ham meat (we like Hormel Naturals)
- 6 pieces cooked bacon
- 6 slices provolone cheese
- Chopped onions and mushrooms if desired
- 6 large tortillas
- 1 cup milk (whole or almond)
- 5 eggs
- Salt and pepper
- Salsa and sour cream

DIRECTIONS:

1. Assemble enchiladas: 3 pieces ham, 1 slice bacon, 1 piece cheese, chopped onions and mushrooms. Roll up.
2. Place in bottom of greased crock (5 quart). Layer as needed.
3. Combine almond milk, eggs, salt and pepper. Whisk.
4. Pour egg mixture over tortillas. Press down lightly. Cover and refrigerate overnight.
5. Cook on HIGH for 1½-2 hours or until eggs are set in the middle.
6. Serve with salsa and sour cream.

Yield: 3-6 servings

Notes:
- You can vary the deli meat based on what you like. Turkey is also a yummy choice.
- The best crock for this is one with a nice wide, flat base so you can put more wraps on the bottom layer. If you need to stack, no biggie, but it may require longer cooking.
- If scrubbing cooked eggs off crocks makes you lose your religion, you might consider a crock liner for this one.

These breakfast enchiladas are a creative new way to enjoy a hearty, warm breakfast. Packed with flavor, these will satisfy even the hungriest of people. The "sauce" was my favorite part. Thanks for taking the boring out of breakfast, Stacy!
++Sarah: Simple Life Abundant Life

Breakfast

Chocolate Peanut Butter Steel Cut Oats

My mom doesn't like peanut butter for breakfast, but I sure do! Sometimes I think I might be adopted…but then Barry tells me, "You're just like your Mama." So I guess maybe my mom just has a flawed breakfast logic. Poor soul. This combination of chocolate and peanut butter with oats might be one of the most genius ideas I ever had. Sorry, Mama.

INGREDIENTS:

- 1 cup steel cut oats
- 3 cups water
- 1 cup milk (whole or almond)
- ¼ cup cocoa powder
- ¼ cup peanut flour (or PB2 or natural peanut butter)
- Pinch of salt
- ¼ cup maple syrup
- 1 teaspoon vanilla extract
- ½ teaspoon butter extract
- Toppings: peanut butter, Greek yogurt, nuts, fresh fruit, dried fruit, etc.

DIRECTIONS:

1. Find a baking dish that is small enough to fit down inside your largest crock with room around the edges. For me, this is a 6 cup bowl in a 6 quart crock.
2. Grease baking dish.
3. Combine all ingredients, except toppings, in baking dish.
4. Set dish inside crock and fill outside edges (NOT IN THE BOWL) with water until it's about ¾ the way up the side of your baking dish.
5. Cover and cook on low 6-8 hours. Stir before serving.
6. Serve alone or with toppings.

Yield: 4 servings

Notes:
- I like really sweet oatmeal…so I sprinkle extra stevia on top of mine. Barry does not. Sweeten to desired likeness and be cool like me.
- If you don't have butter extract, invest in some. It's life changing.
- This might leak a little over the sides and down into the crock. No worries. It cleans easily!
- For my Candida friends, Nature's Hollow makes a maple syrup with xylitol. You can find more details on the _Keep Crockin' Reference Page_.

Who would have thought that peanut butter and chocolate would be so good for breakfast? When you try Stacy's recipe you will be delighted find nourishment that tastes like a chocolate peanut buttercup! This is a fun breakfast for the kid in all of us!
++Katie Mae: _Nourishing Simplicity_

Breakfast

Pumpkin Chip Breakfast Pudding

This was originally an experiment – an idea that I got into my head. It could have totally bombed... but guess what? Instead of bombing, it was THE BOMB. Oh my gosh. It's like Thanksgiving in my mouth – at breakfast – with chocolate. It's a miracle. God bless us, every one.

INGREDIENTS:

- ½ cup melted butter
- 1 cup sugar/xylitol/sucanat
- 2 eggs
- 1 teaspoon vanilla
- 1 (15 ounce) can pumpkin puree (not pie mix)
- 1 cup almond flour (white wheat flour will also work)
- ½ cup ground flax meal
- 1 teaspoon cinnamon
- ¼ teaspoon ginger
- ¼ teaspoon nutmeg
- 1 teaspoon baking soda
- ¼ teaspoon salt
- ¼ cup chocolate chips

DIRECTIONS:

1. Combine butter and sugar.
2. Add eggs, vanilla, and pumpkin. Mix well.
3. Add almond flour, flax, cinnamon, ginger, nutmeg, baking soda, salt, and chocolate chips. Stir until combined.
4. Pour into greased 8 inch bread pan or baking dish that will fit down inside your largest crock. Place baking dish or pan into crock.
5. Pour 2 cups water down the side around edges into the crock – NOT THE PAN.
6. Cover top of crock with a tea towel. This is to trap condensation.
7. Put lid on and cook on HIGH for 2½-3 hours or until toothpick inserted in center comes out clean.
8. Remove pan from crock and let cool 20 minutes.
9. Scoop out warm and serve in bowls with yogurt and berries.

Yield: 6 servings

Notes:
- This is also EXCELLENT served cold out of the fridge.
- This could be a dessert...but I like calling it breakfast. Makes me feel cool.

This breakfast pudding is so delicious and filling! What a perfect way to start the day!

++Jill: Jill's Home Remedies

Breakfast

Basic Baked Oatmeal

This is a variation of one of my most popular posts – *Baked Oatmeal*. I converted it to be cooked in the crock after being soaked overnight. It's fabulous, if I do say so myself. This is the basic recipe so you can tweak it to your heart's content. It's pretty much mind blowing – you're welcome. Get out of your oatmeal rut…it's lonely in there.

INGREDIENTS:

- 2 cups rolled oats
- 1 cup milk (whole or almond)
- 2½ tablespoons Truvia (*I use homemade*) or ½ cup sugar/sucanat
- 2 egg whites (⅓ cup)
- ¼ cup Greek yogurt
- 1½ teaspoons baking powder
- ½ teaspoon salt
- 1 teaspoon vanilla
- ½ teaspoon cinnamon
- Add-ins and Toppings

DIRECTIONS:

1. Combine all ingredients, except toppings. Stir in desired add-ins (see notes).
2. Pour into GREASED crock (4-5 quart).
3. Refrigerate 8 hours or overnight.
4. Cook on HIGH for 1½-2 hours or until set in the middle.
5. Serve with desired toppings.

Yield: 4 servings

Notes:
- Optional add-ins: chopped fruit, berries, chocolate chips, nuts, flavorings and spices, pumpkin or pureed squash, cocoa powder, etc.
- Optional toppings: maple syrup, Greek yogurt, jam, coconut oil, whipped cream
- I have not tried doubling this recipe, but it should work fine. You may have to adjust the cooking time.

This baked oatmeal turned out to be the perfect consistency and with just the right touch of sweetness.
++MaryEllen Bream: Imperfect Homemaker

Breakfast

Soups

Curried Chicken Soup

I'm kinda afraid of curry. I don't eat it often, because I'm afraid I won't like it. But then I do eat it and love it. So, I make no sense. I don't like leaving my comfort zone – I like staying here with my peanut butter and chocolate...but curry can come visit sometimes.

INGREDIENTS:

- 1 pound boneless chicken breast, diced
- 1 onion, chopped (about 1 cup)
- 2 stalks celery, chopped (about 1 cup)
- ½ cup chopped carrots
- 2 cups chicken broth
- 1 teaspoon salt
- 1 teaspoon curry powder
- ¼ teaspoon pepper
- ¼ teaspoon turmeric
- ¼ teaspoon dry mustard
- ½ cup milk (whole or almond)
- 1½ tablespoons cornstarch/arrowroot

DIRECTIONS:

1. In a crock (4 quart), combine chicken, onion, celery, carrots, broth, salt, curry, pepper, turmeric, and dry mustard.
2. Cover and cook on low for 8 hours.
3. Combine milk and cornstarch/arrowroot. Stir into soup.
4. Cover and let thicken 20-30 minutes.

Yield: 3-4 servings

Notes:
- This is a mild curry taste. Feel free to increase if desired or use hot curry for added heat.
- You may thicken this with glucomannan. Start with 1 teaspoon, dissolved in milk like cornstarch.
- If you have a hearty appetite, you may want to double or triple this recipe.

My husband keeps telling me he doesn't like curry, too, but he has loved everything I've made from Stacy's first book, so I tried this. "Really good," he says. "It's curry," I say. "Huh..." comes the quizzical look. This recipe is the definition of fast food for me, thank you Stacy!
++Katie: Kitchen Stewardship

Broccoli Cheese Soup

So yeah—in my first crock pot cookbook I told y'all I didn't like cheese in my broccoli or potato soup. Then I developed this recipe and I changed my tune. This recipe pretty much rocks. So, I stand corrected. I like a little crow with my soup.

INGREDIENTS:

- 24 ounces frozen broccoli cuts or fresh
- 1 small onion, chopped
- ½ cup water
- 1 teaspoon salt
- ½ teaspoon parsley
- ¼ teaspoon pepper
- 1½ cups water
- 1 cup sour cream
- 4 ounces cream cheese, cubed
- 2 cups shredded cheddar
- Chopped, cooked bacon as a garnish

DIRECTIONS:

1. Combine broccoli, onion, ½ cup water, salt, parsley, and pepper in crock (4 quart).
2. Cover and cook on low 4 hours.
3. Remove mixture, add 1½ cups water, and puree in food processor – or puree in the crock with water and an immersion blender.
4. Return mixture to crock.
5. Add sour cream, cream cheese, and shredded cheddar.
6. Cover and let cook an additional hour on low.
7. Whisk to mix cheeses.
8. Serve each bowl with chopped cooked bacon.

Yield: 4-5 servings

Notes:
- Do not skip the bacon. Maybe skip the broccoli, but don't leave out the bacon.
- Try subbing all of the broccoli for cauliflower. I heart cauliflower.

This soup was super easy to put together. And the shorter cooking time means that even if I forget to start it until lunchtime, it will still be ready by suppertime. And it tastes every bit as good as the broccoli cheese soup from my favorite restaurant. Actually it's better because I know exactly what went into it! ++Rachel: Rachel's Ramblings

Soups

Mexican Turkey and Rice Soup

I'm still not sure how I feel about ground turkey – it looks all white and naked when it's raw. And yet, I still keep buying it and using it. I know some of y'all are hog wild and pig crazy about ground turkey—and so I bring you this recipe. And now I'm distracted by the word "hog." Did someone say bacon?

INGREDIENTS:

- 1 pound lean ground turkey
- ½ cup chopped onion
- 1 small green pepper, seeded and chopped
- 1½ cups cooked black beans OR 1 can rinsed and drained
- 1 can (14.5 ounces) diced tomatoes
- 1 can (4 ounces) diced green chilies
- 1 cup tomato sauce (8 ounces)
- 1 cup brown rice
- 4½ cups water
- 2 teaspoons chili powder
- 2 teaspoons cumin
- 1 teaspoon salt
- 1 teaspoon paprika
- ¼ teaspoon pepper

DIRECTIONS:

1. Brown turkey and drain if needed.
2. Combine all ingredients in crock (4 quart).
3. Cover and cook on low 4-6 hours or until rice is done.
4. Serve with tortilla chips.

Yield: 6 servings

Notes:
- If you need to cook this longer than the recommended time, just remove the rice and only use 1-2 cups of water. Add cooked rice at the end of your cooking time instead.
- If you cook longer, say 8 hours, with the rice, don't worry. It will still be tasty, but a tad bit on the mushy side. I have no idea how I would know that though. Ahem.

The Mexican Turkey and Rice Soup recipe was a hit! It had just enough heat to provide the real Mexican flavor but it was quite savory and hearty as well. I had everything in the crock pot and cooking in about 25 minutes. 5 hours later...Voila! A great soup for a cold night.

++Keren: Stepping It Down

White Bean and Ham Soup

Beans! Beans! The magical fruit! The more you eat, the more you errrrrrrrr. Nevermind. And no, I didn't mean "musical fruit." Yes, toots are somewhat musical... but for me, they are more magical because of how you feel afterwards. Dude – this convo is going south fast. Let's end it here.

INGREDIENTS:

- 1 pound dried white beans (I like Navy beans)
- 8 ounces chopped, cooked lean ham pieces
- 1 small onion, chopped
- 1 cup celery, chopped
- 1 teaspoon salt
- 1 teaspoon garlic powder
- ½ teaspoon thyme
- ½ teaspoon pepper
- 5 cups water
- Green onions, sliced if desired

DIRECTIONS:

1. Rinse beans and soak overnight.
2. Drain. Cover with water, bring to a boil in a saucepan. Boil 5 minutes.
3. Drain again.
4. Add beans to a crock (4-5 quart) with ham, onion, celery, salt, garlic, thyme, pepper and water.
5. Cover and cook on low 8 hours.
6. Serve with chopped green onions, if desired.

Yield: 5-6 servings

Notes:
- You could make this with any type of bean...I just like white beans paired with ham. Actually, I wouldn't use peanuts to make this soup. Did you know peanuts were legumes? Yeah – mind blowing.
- This makes EXCELLENT baby food when pureed. Just ask Andy.

This was a wonderful, hearty soup that the whole family loved! There was plenty for our family of 4 to have leftovers and it tasted great the second time, too!
++Heidi: Heidi's @ Home

Soups

Lentil Lasagna Soup

Lentils are a lovely stand-in for meat when you need to stretch your budget. But let's not be silly here – they taste nothing like meat. Nothing at all. In fact, to tell yourself they are meat is just a lie. Liars shall be fryers. Revelation 21:8 Look it up.

INGREDIENTS:

- 1 cup dried lentils, rinsed and looked over
- ½ cup chopped onion
- 1 small pepper, seeded and chopped
- 1 can (14.5 ounce) diced tomatoes
- 1 teaspoon salt
- 1 teaspoon garlic powder
- 1 teaspoon Italian seasoning
- 4 cups beef broth (or vegetable broth)
- 1 cup uncooked rotini pasta
- ¼ cup Parmesan cheese

DIRECTIONS:

1. Combine lentils, onion, pepper, tomatoes, seasonings, and broth in a crock (4-5 quart).
2. Cover and cook on low for 8 hours.
3. Add pasta during last hour of cooking.
4. Stir in Parmesan at end of cooking.
5. Serve topped with additional cheese, if desired.

Yield: 4-5 servings

Notes:
- You can use a combination of lentil types – I like a brown and green mix.
- Other pastas can be used, I just like the swirlies of rotini. It's fun to chew.

Stacy is right; lentils may not taste like meat, but they are very yummy and filling in this soup! My four year old, when I asked her if she liked it, exclaimed "Like it? I love it!" Win! ++Kristen: Smithspirations

Soups

Pork Stir-Fry Soup

When I first decided to concoct this recipe, Barry snarled up his nose and made a nasty face. Then he came home to a house that smelled like heaven and he downed his bowl of soup lickety-split. He said "You were right, honey." I love being right. Booya.

INGREDIENTS:

- 1½ pounds boneless pork, cubed
- 3 tablespoons soy sauce/liquid aminos/coconut aminos
- 24 ounces stir-fry veggies of your choice (about 6 cups) – broccoli, cauliflower, celery, squash, peas, peppers, onions, water chestnuts, etc.
- Salt to taste
- ½ teaspoon garlic powder
- ½ teaspoon ground ginger
- ½ teaspoon pepper
- 2 cups beef broth
- Toasted sesame seeds for serving

DIRECTIONS:

1. Combine all (except seeds) in crock (5 quart).
2. Cover and cook on low 8 hours.
3. Serve each bowl with toasted sesame seeds.

Yield: 5 servings

Notes:
- To make this even more stir-fry-like, add cooked rice to your soup at the end OR put cooked rice in the bottom of each bowl and ladle soup over top.
- Switch it up and make this with different types of meat.

I knew everyone liked this recipe when we had a quiet meal. And everyone got seconds! No leftovers after this meal. If we weren't on GAPS, I would have served it with rice or quinoa. ++Eileen: Wellness and Workouts

Soups

Pizza Chili

Chili is such a wonderful comfort food – and so is pizza. So, I combined them both to make the most amazing chili in the entire world. It's pizza in a bowl, y'all. I know, I know. Your mind just can't take much more crockawesomeness.

INGREDIENTS:

- 1 pound ground beef
- 1 green pepper, chopped
- ½ cup chopped onion
- 2 teaspoons Italian seasoning
- 1 teaspoon garlic salt (or ½ teaspoon salt + ½ teaspoon garlic powder)
- 2 (8 ounce) cans tomato sauce (or 2 cups)
- 1 (14.5 ounce) can diced tomatoes
- 1½ cups water
- 1½ cups cooked kidney beans (one can, rinsed and drained)
- ⅓ cup chopped pepperoni
- ¼ cup chopped black olives
- 1 can mushrooms (4 ounce), drained
- 3 tablespoons Parmesan cheese

DIRECTIONS:

1. Brown meat in a skillet. Drain fat.
2. In a crock (5 quart), combine all ingredients.
3. Cover and cook on low for 8 hours.

Yield: 6 servings

Notes:
- We like turkey pepperoni best. And I really like this dish made with ground venison…it's my ground "beef" of choice.
- Add any additional pizza toppings that you like. Anything goes! And so does this…down the hatch.

My kids love pizza, and my husband loves chili. So, I figured this recipe would be a big hit. Judging from the lack of left overs we had, it was! I will most definitely be making this again! ++Lexie: Lexie Naturals

Loaded Butternut Soup

Every once in a while I come up with a recipe that just knocks my socks off. This is one of those. Yes, I realize the name sounds a little iffy…but trust me, this is a culinary delight that will tickle your taste buds. Ha, ha! That was fun to say – try it.

INGREDIENTS:

- 1 medium butternut squash, peeled, seeded and cubed
- 2 cups chicken broth
- ½ cup onion, chopped
- 1 teaspoon salt
- ½ teaspoon pepper
- ½ cup heavy cream
- ½ cup sour cream
- Chopped, cooked bacon
- Shredded cheese
- Sour cream
- Sliced green onion

DIRECTIONS:

1. Put cubed squash, broth, onion, salt and pepper in crock (4-5 quart).
2. Cover and cook on low 6-8 hour or until squash is tender.
3. Puree soup mixture with immersion blender or use a food processor. Return mixture to crock.
4. Stir in cream and sour cream. Let warm.
5. Serve each bowl topped with bacon, cheese, sour cream, and green onions.

Yield: 5-6 servings

Notes:
- Pumpkin or acorn squash would also work. Use about 8 cups cubed squash of your desire.
- Greek yogurt could stand in for the sour cream.

Every year I grow butternut squash in my garden but very few recipes I actually make with it. Believe me, this recipe didn't disappoint. I loved how easy the soup was to make in the crock pot and how rich, creamy, and delicious it was. This recipe is definitely a keeper and I can't wait to make it again. ++Jackie: _Blessings Overflowing_

Soups

Chicken Taco Soup

I like my soup spicy, but alas, this isn't overly spicy as written – my 4 year old freaks out if something is spicy. Spice it up if you need to. "Some like it hot, some like it cold. Some like it in the pot, 9 days old." Does that song sound dumb to anyone else? Who eats 9 day old soup straight from the pot? Lame.

INGREDIENTS:

- 1½ pounds chicken tenders
- ½ cup chopped onion
- 2 cans (14.5 ounces each) diced tomatoes
- 1 can (4 ounces) diced green chilies
- 1 teaspoon cumin
- 1 teaspoon chili powder
- 1 teaspoon paprika
- ½ teaspoon salt
- ½ teaspoon garlic powder
- ¼ teaspoon pepper
- Chopped cilantro, shredded cheese, and/or tortilla chips for serving

DIRECTIONS:

1. Combine all ingredients, except toppings, in a crock (4 quart).
2. Cover and cook on low 8 hours.
3. Remove chicken and shred. Return to crock.
4. Serve each bowl topped with cilantro and shredded cheese. Add tortilla chips if desired.

Yield: 5 servings

Notes:
- Spice things up and add cayenne pepper.
- Sub out the chicken with 1½ pounds ground beef.
- I save time and shred my chicken right in the crock, using two forks.

This soup is so yummy and so easy! The chili peppers add a little kick - which I love. My teenage daughter, a very picky eater, ate three bowls!
++Wendy: Hip Homeschool Moms

Hamburger Stew

This recipe was born when I wanted Beef Stew but had no stew beef in the freezer. I always have plenty of ground venison though. Booya. I could call it Venison Stew, but then you would have skipped right over it. Wouldn't you? Don't lie – your eye is twitching. Use whatever ground meat you like.

INGREDIENTS:

- 1 pound ground beef/venison
- 1 cup chopped carrots
- 1 cup chopped potato or turnip
- 1 cup chopped celery
- 1 small onion, chopped
- 28 ounces crushed tomatoes
- 6 ounces tomato paste
- 1 teaspoon minced garlic
- 1 teaspoon salt
- ½ teaspoon thyme
- ½ teaspoon oregano
- ½ teaspoon pepper

DIRECTIONS:

1. Brown beef in skillet. Drain.
2. Add to crock (4 quart) with remaining ingredients. Stir well.
3. Cover and cook on low for 8 hours.
4. Serve hot with toasted garlic bread or cheese toast.

Yield: 5 servings

Notes:
- If you have stew beef, you can easily use it in place of the ground meat. I would use 1 ½ pounds.
- Our family doesn't eat much potato, so I use cubed chayote squash in place of that for this recipe – it's very tasty.

This savory hamburger stew is perfect for tomato lovers. It was really quick to put together in the morning for a no-fuss dinner, and the whole family went for seconds. A word of caution though: prep time doubles when cooking with a 2-year-old chef.
++Shannon: GrowingSlower

Soups

Main Dishes

Pizza Sandwiches

I love Sloppy Joes... and it's hard to improve upon their beauty and messiness. Until you try these. You might never go back to regular Sloppy Joes again. Sorry school cafeteria – you lose.

INGREDIENTS:

- 1 pound ground breakfast sausage
- 1 6 ounce can tomato paste
- ¾ cup water
- ½ cup chopped onion
- ½ cup chopped green pepper
- 4 ounce can mushrooms, drained or ½ cup chopped fresh
- 2 teaspoons Italian seasoning
- 1 teaspoon minced garlic
- 1 teaspoon salt
- ½ teaspoon oregano
- ½ teaspoon black pepper
- Buns, if desired
- Shredded mozzarella

DIRECTIONS:

1. Brown sausage in skillet. Drain.
2. Add tomato paste and water to crock. Whisk to combine.
3. Stir in meat, onion, pepper, mushrooms, and seasonings.
4. Cover and cook on low for 6 hours.
5. Serve on buns with mozzarella cheese.

Yield: 6 sandwiches

Notes:
- You can serve this on hamburger buns or in hot dog buns like a chili dog.
- This would also make an excellent pizza topping! Add whatever ingredients you enjoy on your pizza to this lovely dish.

"Booya" ++Stacy-ism

Main Dishes

Chili Dogs in a Bowl

This is one of those recipes that just sorta came to me in the bathroom. I do most of my deep thinking in there – while little people stick their hands under the door and say "Mama! What are you doing in there?!" But really, this recipe is delicious – I could eat the whole crock myself.

© 2013 Stacy Myers | Keep Crockin' | Stacy Makes Cents

INGREDIENTS:

- 2 pounds ground meat (I use venison)
- ½ cup chopped onion
- 1 pound hot dogs, sliced
- 16 ounces (2 cups) tomato sauce
- 1 (14.5 ounce) can diced tomatoes
- 1 cup water
- 1½ tablespoons chili powder
- 2 tablespoons sugar/xylitol/sucanat
- 2 tablespoons prepared mustard
- 1 teaspoon salt
- ½ teaspoon pepper

DIRECTIONS:

1. Brown meat and onion in skillet. Drain.
2. In crock (5 quart), combine all ingredients. Stir well.
3. Cover and cook on low for 8 hours.
4. Serve as is, or in a bun using a slotted spoon to get chili out.

Yield: 6-8 servings

Notes:
- We use nitrate free hot dogs. I LOVE the chicken ones from Trader Joes.
- Serve in a bowl with extra mustard on top – and anything else you'd normally put on your chili dog.

This is so good! It took all of the self-control I could muster to NOT pour this over a big 'ol pile of Fritos. My kids call this "Hot Dog Chili" and it has quickly become a staple in our house-full of little kids!
++Nikki: Christian Mommy Blogger

Main Dishes

Chicken Stroganoff

I love beef, but sometimes a girl needs to get her chicken on - and keep the 4 year old happy...who happens to like chicken better. Weird, I know she's not adopted, but I can't explain that one.

INGREDIENTS:

- 1½ pounds boneless, skinless chicken breast, cubed
- 1 medium onion, chopped
- 2 cups chicken broth
- ½ teaspoon minced garlic
- ½ teaspoon dried rosemary
- ½ teaspoon dried parsley
- 1 tablespoon tomato paste
- 1 (4 ounce) can mushrooms, drained
- 1 cup sour cream
- 3 tablespoons cornstarch
- 3 tablespoons water
- Quinoa or rice for serving

DIRECTIONS:

1. Place chicken in bottom of crock (4 quart).
2. Place onion on top of chicken.
3. In a bowl, combine chicken broth, garlic, rosemary, parsley and tomato paste.
4. Pour broth over chicken.
5. Cover and cook on low for 8 hours.
6. Add mushrooms and sour cream.
7. Thicken with cornstarch mixed with water. Let stand until desired thickness.
8. Serve over quinoa or rice...cooked, of course.

Yield: 5 servings

Notes:
- What to do with the rest of the tomato paste? Freeze in ice cube trays for recipes like this that only call for 1 tablespoon.
- Or you can be a rebel like me. I like to always keep paste in the fridge for a quick tortilla pizza. Spread it on the tortilla, sprinkle with Italian seasoning. BAM! Instant pizza sauce folks!
- You can also thicken this by sprinkling 1 teaspoon of glucomannan over the mixture and whisking well to avoid clumping.

I love it because it's simple to prepare and the flavor is such that any vegetable or salad complements it well. And the kids like it too....that's the ultimate test.

++Jacinda: Growing Home

Main Dishes

Thai Chicken

I like food that makes my nose run. My 4 year old does not. So, I have to make sure our food isn't overly hot for her. If you want to sweat and cry at dinner, make sure to up the cayenne in this dish – or just eat dinner in a sauna while watching a sad movie.

INGREDIENTS:

- 1 pound chicken, sliced into strips
- 1 cup chicken broth
- 3 tablespoons soy sauce
- 2 tablespoons peanut butter
- 1 tablespoon toasted sesame oil (optional, but delish!)
- ⅛-¼ teaspoon cayenne pepper (adjust to your liking – more if you like lots of heat)
- 1 onion, sliced
- 2 green peppers, seeded and sliced
- Salt and Pepper to taste
- 2 tablespoons cornstarch or arrowroot
- 2 tablespoons water
- Rice
- Toasted Sesame Seeds

DIRECTIONS:

1. Place chicken in crock (4 quart).
2. Combine broth, soy sauce, peanut butter, oil, and cayenne pepper. Pour over chicken.
3. Lay onion and pepper on top.
4. Cover and cook on low for 6 hours.
5. Combine cornstarch and water. Stir into juices. Cover and let thicken (about 5-10 minutes).
6. Serve over rice

Yield: 4 servings

Notes:
- At ⅛ tsp cayenne it's just barely spicy. Start with that and add more if you like a lot of heat
- I served with cauliflower rice (cauliflower that's cooked and processed until it looks like rice).
- You can also thicken this by sprinkling ½-1 teaspoon of glucomannan over the mixture and whisking well to avoid clumping.

While I am all about trying new foods, my children are not. The Thai Chicken smelled so yummy cooking in the crock pot all day, I couldn't wait to eat dinner. I served the chicken over rice and everyone cleaned their plates. I call that a success!
++Whitney: Beauty in the Mess

Main Dishes

Popover Pizza

This is a crock pot take on one of my Mama's recipes. Except hers calls for double the amount of breading...but if you've known me for long, you know I like MEAT. Meat, baby, meat. Give me the meat. Also, I cut back on the cheese amount and converted it to almond flour. It pretty much rocks the crock.

INGREDIENTS:

- 1 pound ground sausage
- 1 large onion, diced
- 1 large green pepper, diced
- 1 (4 ounce) can mushrooms, drained
- 1 (15 ounce) can diced tomatoes, drained
- 1 (8 ounce) can tomato sauce
- Dash stevia
- 2 teaspoons Italian seasoning
- 1 teaspoon minced garlic
- ¼ teaspoon salt
- Pepperoni
- 1 cup mozzarella cheese, shredded
- ⅔ cup almond flour
- 1 teaspoon baking powder
- ½ teaspoon salt
- ½ cup almond milk
- 2 eggs

DIRECTIONS:

1. Brown sausage in a skillet with mushrooms, onions and green peppers. Drain.
2. Pour meat into crock (4 quart) along with tomatoes, tomato sauce, stevia, garlic, Italian seasoning, and salt.
3. Cover and cook on low 4 hours.
4. Uncover and sprinkle top with pepperoni and mozzarella.
5. In a mixing bowl, combine almond flour, baking powder, salt, milk, and eggs. Whisk well.
6. Pour over meat mixture.
7. Cover and cook on HIGH for 1½-2 hours or until knife inserted in center comes out clean.

Yield: 5 servings

Notes:
- You can use regular flour for this recipe in the same quantity, but just take out the baking powder.
- Add any pizza toppings you like as you're adding the pepperoni: olives, pineapple, ham, bacon, etc.

This is the perfect game day or race day dinner. It's much healthier than delivery and the topping options are endless. We did bacon and extra mushrooms, it was delicious! ++Danielle: *More Than Four Walls*

Main Dishes

Yummy Dill Beef Roast

I'm not sure what else to call this. It's yummy. It's pot roast. There ya go. If you don't care for the flavor of dill, then leave it out. I just threw it in on a whim and we really liked it. I wouldn't leave the meat out though...then this would just be titled "Yummy Herbs".

INGREDIENTS:

- 3 pound beef roast (we like rump roast)
- 1 tablespoon parsley
- 1 tablespoon oregano
- 2 teaspoons salt
- 1½ teaspoons garlic powder
- 1 teaspoon dried dill
- 1 teaspoon onion powder
- 1 teaspoon pepper
- 1 teaspoon dried basil
- 1 teaspoon dried minced onion
- ½ teaspoon dried thyme
- ½ teaspoon celery salt
- ½ cup beef broth
- 1 tablespoon cornstarch/arrowroot
- 1 tablespoon water

DIRECTIONS:

1. Place roast in bottom of a crock (5 quart).
2. In a small bowl, combine parsley, oregano, salt, garlic, dill, pepper, basil, minced onion, thyme and celery salt.
3. Rub spice mixture into meat on all sides.
4. Pour ½ cup beef broth into bottom of crock.
5. Cover and cook on low for 8 hours or until roast is done in middle (generally when internal temp is 160° F).
6. Remove roast from crock.
7. Combine cornstarch and water. Stir into juices. Cover and let thicken (about 10-15 minutes)
8. Serve gravy over roast.

Yield: 6 servings

Notes:
- If you don't use cornstarch, arrowroot is an acceptable alternative.
- This would be DIVINE served on a hoagie roll with gravy poured all over. Wait...gravy. I love gravy.
- You can also thicken this by sprinkling ½-1 teaspoon of glucomannan over the juices and whisking well to avoid clumping.

The roast was delish! I'm not typically a huge fan of roast, but this was fall-apart tender and super flavorful. I'll definitely be keeping this recipe handy.
++ Trisha: Intoxicated on Life

Main Dishes

Sweet and Spicy Boston Butt

I like big butts and I cannot lie...pork butts. There is just something beautiful about a nice, big round butt that fits perfectly down into my crock. I like to rub the butt with spices. Don't worry about the fat on your butt – you can take it off later. HAHAHAHAHAHA! Okay, sorry. Enough butt jokes.

INGREDIENTS:

- 4 pound Boston butt roast
- 1 large onion, sliced
- Salt
- 2 cups beef stock
- 1 tablespoon Bragg's Liquid Aminos or soy sauce
- 1 teaspoon garlic powder
- 1 teaspoon chili powder
- ½-1 teaspoon cayenne pepper
- ½ teaspoon cumin
- ½ teaspoon dry mustard
- ½ teaspoon smoked paprika
- 6 ounces tomato paste
- ⅛-¼ teaspoon stevia extract powder OR 2 tablespoons-⅓ cup sugar/xylitol/sucanat
- 1 cup chicken stock
- Buns, rice, etc. for serving

DIRECTIONS:

1. Place sliced onion in bottom of crock. I use my 6 quart for butts...big butts need big pants.
2. Place butt on top. Salt as desired.
3. Pour in beef stock.
4. Cover and cook on low for 8 hours.
5. In a small mixing bowl, combine Braggs, garlic, cumin, mustard, cayenne, chili powder, paprika, tomato paste, stevia extract and stock. Stir until combined.
6. Remove roast from crock and shred. Discard fatty part of butt = no one wants excess butt fat.
7. Drain broth from crock, reserving onions.
8. Stir sauce into meat and add onions.
9. Serve on buns or with rice.

Yield: 8 servings...but it really depends on how fatty your butt is. HAHAHAHAHAHA!

Notes:
- I like a drier sauce with my meat. If you like your butt saucy (HA!) then just double the sauce for this mixture.
- This would also be delish as the meat on a salad. Yum!

This is an excellent recipe that had glowing reviews from the entire family. The mix of sweet and spice was perfect!
++*Shannon: Simply Smiles*

Main Dishes

Italian Meatloaf

I have this thing for meatloaf and meatballs... maybe it's just a thing for meat. Anyway, I'm always coming up with ideas for different flavors of meatloaf. This one did not disappoint. Actually, it did...it was gone way too fast. Get away from my meatloaf before I bite off your finger.

INGREDIENTS:

- 2 pounds ground beef
- ¼ cup oats/almond flour
- 1 tablespoon Italian seasoning
- 1 teaspoon garlic powder
- 1 teaspoon salt
- ½ teaspoon onion powder
- ½ teaspoon pepper
- 1 cup shredded mozzarella cheese
- 1 (14 ounce) can diced tomatoes with basil, drained
- 2 eggs
- ¼ cup Parmesan cheese
- Spaghetti sauce for serving, if desired

DIRECTIONS:

1. Combine all ingredients except Parmesan and spaghetti sauce.
2. Shape into a loaf inside a crock (5 quart).
3. Sprinkle with Parmesan.
4. Cover and cook on low for 7 hours until temp reads 170 degrees.
5. Drain fat if necessary.
6. Serve with spaghetti sauce if desired.

Yield: 6 servings

Notes:
- Shaping into a loaf in your crock creates a "moat" around the outside edges so it's easier to pour off the fat at the end.
- I use ground venison, so I have very little fat to pour off.
- No tomatoes with basil? Just add ½ teaspoon dried basil and use a can of plain tomatoes.

Stacy, this recipe is a keeper! It smelled so great that we could hardly wait to eat it! So flavorful and delicious, one of our older sons said, "Mom, this is meatloaf on steroids!" We loved it!

++Brandy: The Marathon Mom

Main Dishes

Cabbage "Un"rolls

Here is my confession: I've never made cabbage rolls. I'm too stinking lazy. The whole idea of steaming cabbage leaves, peeling them off and then stuffing them with meat mixture makes me want to call and order a pizza. So, I make it this way. I'm lazy. Keepin' it real.

INGREDIENTS:

- 1 pound ground beef
- ½ cup chopped green pepper
- 1 medium onion, chopped
- 2 tablespoons nutritional yeast (optional but GOOD)
- 1 tablespoon soy sauce or Bragg's liquid aminos
- 1 egg
- 2 teaspoons salt
- 2 teaspoons Italian seasoning
- 1 teaspoon pepper
- 1 teaspoon garlic powder
- 1 teaspoon oregano
- 8 ounces tomato sauce
- 2 (14 ounce) cans diced tomatoes, drained
- 1 tablespoon sugar (or one dash NuNaturals stevia)
- 8 cups shredded cabbage
- 2 tablespoons Parmesan cheese
- Shredded cheddar for serving, if desired

DIRECTIONS:

1. Brown meat in a skillet with pepper and onion. Drain fat to get rid of extra liquid.
2. Stir in nutritional yeast, Bragg's, egg, salt, Italian seasoning, pepper, garlic powder, and oregano.
3. Add tomatoes, tomato sauce, and sugar (stevia). Stir until combined.
4. In the bottom of a crock (5 quart), pour ½ meat sauce.
5. Cover with cabbage.
6. Top with remaining sauce.
7. Sprinkle with Parmesan cheese.
8. Cover and cook on low for 8 hours.
9. Top with cheddar if desired and serve with slotted spoon.

Yield: 5 servings

Notes:
- This will seem like a LOT of cabbage, but it will cook down by at least half. No worries.
- If you're buying cabbage and not shredding if yourself, this is the same as two 10 ounce packages shredded cabbage.

This recipe was good, and worked. I'll probably serve it over rice when I make it again; my baby (19 months) ate 3 bowls!!
++Katie: Simple Foody

Main Dishes

Chicken "Slop"

I thought I was being real smart with this recipe. I originally called it "Kickin' Chicken." Until someone informed me that name had already been taken. Oops. So, instead I'll call it Chicken Slop. Because, that's kinda what it looks like. It is what it is. But it tastes GOOD.

INGREDIENTS:

- 2 pounds chicken tenders
- 1 cup chopped green peppers (2 fresh)
- 2 (14 ounce) cans diced tomatoes, drained
- 1 can (4 ounce) diced green chilies
- 1 teaspoon salt
- 1 teaspoon chili powder
- ½ teaspoon minced garlic
- ½ teaspoon pepper
- ¼ teaspoon cayenne (increase if you like it HOT)
- 8 ounce cream cheese, cubed
- Rice, Noodles, or Tortilla Chips
- Shredded Cheese
- 1-2 tablespoons of cornstarch + 1-2 tablespoons water

DIRECTIONS:

1. Place chicken in bottom of crock (4 quart).
2. Combine peppers, tomatoes, chilies, salt, chili powder, garlic, pepper and cayenne.
3. Pour mixture over chicken.
4. Cover and cook on low for 8 hours.
5. Add cubed cream cheese, stir, and cover to let melt. Stir occasionally.
6. Shred chicken if desired.
7. Now is the time to thicken if you want – it's not required…depends on what you are serving it with. Combine cornstarch/arrowroot and water. Stir into juices. Cover and let thicken.
8. Serve over rice, noodles, or as a dip with tortilla chips. Top with cheese.

Yield: 6-8 servings

Notes:
- If you desire, you can eat this almost like a soup instead of a meal over rice. Add more broth if you want to go that route.
- This isn't overly hot – so add more cayenne if you want some kick.

This creamy, chicken dish was SO easy to throw together! The added peppers gave it a nice, flavorful kick.
++Sarah: Domestic Femme

Main Dishes

Bourbon Chicken

I don't have anything against bourbon. I just didn't put any in this recipe – but it still reminds me of bourbon chicken. So there. If you want, you can have some bourbon while you eat this...but don't drink and drive – or drink and wash dishes. On second thought – drink and wash dishes.

INGREDIENTS:

- 1½ pounds chicken breast, cubed
- 1 teaspoon salt
- ½ teaspoon garlic powder
- ¼ teaspoon ground ginger
- ¼ teaspoon onion powder
- ¼ teaspoon pepper
- ¾ cup chicken broth
- ¼ cup soy sauce or Bragg Liquid Aminos
- ¼ cup sugar/xylitol/sucanat
- 2 tablespoons sugar-free ketchup
- ½ tablespoon apple cider vinegar
- 2 tablespoons flour
- 2 tablespoons water
- Rice for serving

DIRECTIONS:

1. Place cubed chicken in bottom of your crock (3-4 quart).
2. In a bowl, combine broth, soy sauce, vinegar, ketchup, sucanat, salt, garlic powder, ginger, onion powder, and pepper. Stir well.
3. Pour mixture over chicken.
4. Cover and cook on low for 8 hours.
5. In a small bowl, combine water and flour. Stir into chicken juices.
6. Cover and let thicken (up to 30 minutes).
7. Serve over rice.

Yield: 4-5 servings

Notes:
- If you hate rice, this would be equally delicious over noodles.
- Try cooking your rice in some chicken broth for extra flavor.
- You can also thicken this by sprinkling ½-1 teaspoon of glucomannan over the mixture and whisking well to avoid clumping.

My family loved this sweet and tangy dish! It was easy to put together in the morning using ingredients I had in the pantry and it tasted great with brown rice.
++Lisa: The Home Life (and Me)

Main Dishes

Chicken Jambalaya

Okay, so I hate shrimp. I realize traditional Jambalaya has shrimp and sausage, but you won't find that here. Mainly because shrimp makes me want to yak and I doubt you want to hear about that dinner. And I just don't like sausage in my Jambalaya. Hence the title Chicken Jambalaya. It is what it is.

INGREDIENTS:

- 2 cans (14.5 ounces) diced tomatoes, undrained
- 1 (4 ounce) can diced green chilies
- 8 ounces (1 cup) tomato sauce
- 1 cup water
- 1 cup chopped green pepper
- 1 cup chopped onion
- 1 cup chopped celery
- 1 teaspoon minced garlic
- 1 teaspoon dried basil
- 1 teaspoon oregano
- 2 teaspoons chili powder
- ½ teaspoon paprika
- 1 teaspoon salt
- ½ teaspoon cayenne pepper
- 1½ pounds boneless chicken breast, cubed
- 2 cups cooked brown rice

DIRECTIONS:

1. Combine all ingredients, except rice, in a crock (5 quart).
2. Cover and cook on low 6-7 hours.
3. Stir in cooked rice.
4. Serve in bowls and grab a tissue.

Yield: 6 LARGE servings

Notes:
- You can add shrimp and sausage if you like. Just don't tell me. Add both when the Jambalaya has about 1 hour left to cook.
- These are really big servings. If you don't eat much, then you might get 8 servings from this recipe.

Stacy's Chicken Jambalaya recipe is easy and quick to throw together, and it's a tasty main dish. But yowie! Its spiciness gives it quite a kick.
++Hilary: Accidentally Green

Italian Casserole

Something about Italian food makes me want to sing "That's Amore!" all day long. Because it is love – true love. Pairing meat, noodles, and cheese together? Those Italians, they're genius. Pure genius. If you don't like this recipe, you're not Italian...or human. True dat.

© 2013 Stacy Myers | Keep Crockin' | Stacy Makes Cents

INGREDIENTS:

- 1 pound ground beef
- 1 teaspoon minced garlic
- 1 teaspoon dried basil
- 1 tablespoon Italian seasoning
- 1 teaspoon salt
- ½ teaspoon pepper
- ½ teaspoon onion powder
- 2 (14 ounce) cans diced tomatoes
- 1 6 ounce can tomato paste
- 16 ounces cottage cheese
- 2 eggs
- ½ teaspoon salt
- ¼ teaspoon pepper
- ¼ cup Parmesan cheese
- 4 ounces cream cheese, cubed
- 1 cup shredded cheddar cheese
- 1 cup shredded mozzarella cheese
- 13 ounces (give or take) noodles of your choice (I like linguine), broken into thirds if using spaghetti style noodles

DIRECTIONS:

1. Brown beef. Drain.
2. In the same skillet, add garlic, basil, Italian seasoning, 1 teaspoon salt, ½ teaspoon pepper, and onion powder.
3. Stir in tomatoes and tomato paste until well combined.
4. In a mixing bowl, combine cottage cheese, eggs, ½ teaspoon salt, ¼ teaspoon pepper, Parmesan cheese, cream cheese, cheddar, and mozzarella. Stir well.
5. Layer ⅓ of the meat sauce in the bottom of a crock (5 quart).
6. Cover with half of the noodles.
7. Cover with half cheese mixture.
8. Repeat layers and end with sauce on top.
9. Cover and cook on low for 4-5 hours or until noodles are tender.

Yield: 6-8 servings

Notes:
- Yes, I realize this is almost like lasagna...but it's not. The cream cheese adds a little somethin'-somethin'. Use the other half of the 8 ounce block to make a cream cheese omelet. I'm hungry.
- I buy all my spices in bulk from the local Amish store

My family + my dear brother in law tried the Italian Casserole after church on Sunday. Almost like a lasagna, the Italian casserole is cheesy and delicious. It was simple to put together and everyone cleaned their plates.
++Becca: Phoenix Community Coffee

Main Dishes

Spicy Spaghetti and Meatballs

I have this thing for meatballs – maybe I just have a thing for meat... yeah, that's probably it. But really, I love little balls of delicious meat swimming in sauce. I don't even need noodles – but I do try to appear normal SOME of the time.

INGREDIENTS:

- 2 pounds ground meat
- 1½ teaspoons salt
- ½ teaspoon pepper
- ½ teaspoon cayenne pepper
- ⅓ cup oats/almond flour
- 1 egg
- 1 tablespoon dried minced onion
- 2 (14 ounce) cans diced tomatoes
- 1 (6 ounce) can tomato paste
- 4 ounces diced green chilies
- ½ cup chopped onion
- 1 teaspoon minced garlic
- ¼ cup sugar/xylitol/sucanat
- 2 teaspoons Italian seasoning
- 1 teaspoon salt
- ½ teaspoon cayenne pepper
- Noodles for serving

DIRECTIONS:

1. Combine meat, 1½ teaspoons salt, ½ teaspoon pepper, ½ teaspoon cayenne pepper, oats, egg, and dried minced onion. Mix well.
2. In your crock (5 quart), combine tomatoes, paste, chilies, onion, garlic, sugar, Italian seasoning, 1 teaspoon salt, ½ teaspoon cayenne. Stir well.
3. Form meat into meatballs of desired size. Drop meatballs into sauce.
4. Stir GENTLY to coat meatballs with sauce.
5. Cover and cook on low for 7 hours.
6. Serve over noodles.

Yield: 6-8 servings

Notes:
- If you would like to thicken your sauce, you can do so by combining 1 tablespoon of cornstarch and 1 tablespoon of water. Stir into sauce and let thicken about 20 minutes.
- This would also be delicious served on hoagie rolls as Meatball Subs
- You may use zucchini or squash noodles.

These certainly lived up to their spicy name! The sauce is spicy, sweet, and full of flavor. I could barely wait to eat after smelling that intoxicating aroma all day. My whole family enjoyed this twist on a classic dish, and I loved that it was an easy meal to prepare and clean up as well.
++Tara: We Got Real

Main Dishes

Chicken Tikka Masala

I have always loved this dish...but I haven't always loved the list of spices it calls for. Most of them, the common housewife (that's ME) doesn't have them on hand. I'm all for using what you got, so I converted this traditional recipe using spices I had. Booya. Raise the roof!

INGREDIENTS:

- 1 pound chicken tenders
- 1 cup tomato sauce
- 1 teaspoon cumin
- 1 teaspoon paprika
- 1 teaspoon chili powder
- 1 teaspoon salt
- ½ teaspoon cinnamon
- ½ teaspoon garlic powder
- ½ teaspoon pepper
- ½ teaspoon ginger
- ¼ teaspoon cayenne pepper
- HEAPING ½ cup sour cream
- Rice or quinoa for serving

DIRECTIONS:

1. In crock (4 quart), lay chicken.
2. Combine tomato sauce and spices.
3. Pour over chicken.
4. Cover and cook on low for 4-6 hours.
5. Shred chicken.
6. Stir in sour cream.
7. Serve over rice or quinoa.

Yield: 4 servings

Notes:
- This is a tad spicy...so, remember that when you're cooking. If you like to sweat, just increase the cayenne.
- This would also be excellent served over noodles...but that's not the normal way to serve it. Then again, I'm not normal.

Having lived in India, our family is pretty picky when it comes to Indian food. However, Stacy's Chicken Tikka Masala was not only eaten by the entire family but passed the "close-to-tasting- like TRUE Indian cuisine.
++Jodi: Granola Mom 4 God

Main Dishes

Green Chicken and Quinoa

I do not like Green Chicken and Quinoa, I do not like them Sam I Am. Okay, that totally doesn't work. Nothing rhymes with quinoa! Ack! That's going to bother me forever and ever. Great. But, I do like this dish. I like it, Sam...or whoever you are.

INGREDIENTS:

- 2½ cups chopped tomatillos (little green tomatoes) or 2 cups tomatillo salsa
- 1 pound chicken tenders, cubed
- 1½ cups cooked, rinsed beans (or one can, rinsed and drained)
- 2 jalapeño peppers, seeded and chopped (or 2 tablespoons of the jar variety)
- 1 green pepper, seeded and chopped
- 1 cup chopped onion
- 1 teaspoon cumin
- 1 teaspoon salt
- 1 teaspoon thyme
- 1 teaspoon chili powder
- ½ teaspoon garlic powder
- 1 cup quinoa
- 1½-2½ cups water (quantity needed will depend on how hot your crock cooks... may need to add additional water as it cooks – start with 1½ cups)
- Salsa, if desired

DIRECTIONS:

1. Combine all ingredients in a crock (4 quart).
2. Cover and cook on low 6-8 hours.
3. Top servings with salsa, if desired.

Yield: 5 servings

Notes:
- Tomatillo salsa is also referred to as Salsa Verde (green). Genius, huh? Omit jalapeños if using salsa...unless you don't want to. Fist bump.
- You can use any type of beans you like for this dish...we like Great Northern the best.

At first I was a little skeptical of the quinoa and green salsa combo, but wow! It was amazing! I used just half the chili powder just to keep it mild for the kids, and topped with a dollop of sour cream. So yummy! I'll definitely be making this again!
++Jessica: Smarter Each Day

Main Dishes

Buffalo Chicken Lasagna

Do you like your nose to run at the dinner table? I do...unless it's allergy related – then that's totally not cool. But buffalo nose run? Yes please. It's not hot enough if you don't need a hanky. Amen.

INGREDIENTS:

- 7 lasagna noodles, uncooked
- 2 tablespoons butter
- 8 ounces cream cheese, cubed
- ½ teaspoon minced garlic
- 1 teaspoon salt
- ½ teaspoon pepper
- 1 cup buffalo sauce (recipe for homemade version available on _References page_ – make "healthier" substitutions)
- 1 cup sour cream
- 3 cups chopped, cooked chicken breast
- 2 cups cottage cheese
- 1 egg
- ¼ cup Parmesan cheese
- Salt and pepper to taste
- 2 cups mozzarella
- Parmesan for topping

DIRECTIONS:

1. In a saucepan, melt butter. Add cream cheese, garlic, salt and pepper. Stir constantly until melted. Remove from heat.
2. Stir in buffalo sauce and sour cream. Add chicken and stir.
3. In a small bowl, combine cottage cheese, egg, ¼ cup Parmesan, and salt and pepper. Stir well.
4. Layer as follows in a GREASED crock (5 quart): sauce, noodles (break to fit), cottage cheese mixture, mozzarella, sauce, noodles, cottage cheese mixture, mozzarella, noodles, cottage cheese mixture, remaining sauce and top with Parmesan cheese.
5. Cover and cook on low for 4 hours OR high for 2 hours.

Yield: 6-8 servings

Notes:
- Honesty? I don't make my own hot sauce. I buy it. Keepin' it real.
- You can tone down the heat by using less hot sauce. Replace missing sauce with heavy cream.

This recipe was easy to assemble (I did it the night before) and it cooked up in 2 hours on high. I left it on warm after that because we weren't quite ready for dinner and it was fine to sit there for another 45 minutes like that. Overall, we loved and I will definitely make it again!   ++ Kailyn: A New (England) Life

Main Dishes

Salisbury Steak

When I first came home with Annie from the hospital, I was a ravenous beast. And I wanted Salisbury Steak all the time – my mom's version. This is nothing like that version, but it's just as good. So I'm not sure why I just told you that story. Oh well.

INGREDIENTS:

- 1 pound ground beef
- 2 teaspoons dried minced onion
- 1 teaspoon dried parsley
- 1 teaspoon garlic powder
- ½ teaspoon onion powder
- ½ teaspoon celery salt
- ½ teaspoon salt
- ¼ teaspoon pepper
- ¼ cup almond flour or breadcrumbs
- ¼ cup milk of choice
- 1 cup beef broth
- ½ cup sour cream
- 1 tablespoon cornstarch/arrowroot + 1 tablespoon water

DIRECTIONS:

1. Combine beef, minced onion, parsley, garlic, onion powder, celery salt, salt, pepper, almond flour, and milk.
2. Form into 5 patties.
3. Place in bottom of crock (5 quart). If you double the recipe, stack the patties off center of each other.
4. Pour broth over patties.
5. Cover and cook on low 6-8 hours.
6. Remove patties.
7. Stir in sour cream with a whisk.
8. Combine cornstarch and water in a small bowl. Stir into broth mixture.
9. Return patties to liquid. Cover and let thicken.
10. Serve patties with gravy.

Yield: 4 servings

Notes:
- This recipe easily doubles. Just stack the patties off center in your crock.
- A crock pot with a wide bottom base works best for this. I use my 5 quart.
- Serve over noodles or mashed potatoes...or plain like me.

This recipe was delish! Good flavor to the meat patties and the gravy... So savory!

++Tanya: Lolo Moku

Salsa Lime Beef

I think my love of beef started when I was very young and used to sport my "Where's The Beef" t-shirt. I really can't get enough. I could eat it every day. I think vegetarians must have never had a GOOD piece of beef. And if you're vegetarian reading this, my apologies and don't send me hate mail.

INGREDIENTS:

- 2 pounds stew beef
- 2 tablespoons soy sauce or Bragg's Liquid Aminos
- Juice from one lime (about ¼ cup)
- Remaining lime, quartered
- ½ cup salsa
- 1 tablespoon cornstarch + 1 tablespoon water
- Mashed potatoes/cauliflower

DIRECTIONS:

1. Place beef in bottom of crock.
2. Add soy sauce, lime juice, limes, and salsa.
3. Cover and cook on low for 6-8 hours.
4. Remove lime.
5. Add cornstarch/water mixture. Stir and cover to thicken.
6. Serve over mashed potatoes or cauliflower.

Yield: 5-6 servings

Notes:
- If you want a milder lime flavor, remove lime after 4 hours of cooking instead of the full 6-8.
- This would also be excellent with cubed pork loin…but not cubed tofu. *Shudder* Again, no hate mail.
- If mashed potatoes don't float your boat, serve this over some brown rice.
- You can also thicken this by sprinkling ½ teaspoon of glucomannan over the mixture and whisking well to avoid clumping.

This was a new and unique dish for us. The combination of lime juice and salsa works perfectly to tenderize the stew meat even more than usual, and it comes out very tender. This yummy recipe will definitely go in my "go-to recipe" box!
++Becca: C Family of 6

Main Dishes

Teriyaki Chicken

I love any chicken dish I can eat with rice. For me, this dish rivals the Maple Sesame Chicken in Crock On...it might even be better than that. It's salty and delicious and salty. I love salt. Yum. It's so good. I love salt – did I say that already?

INGREDIENTS:

- 1½ pounds chicken breast, cubed
- ½ cup soy sauce or Bragg Liquid Aminos
- 2 tablespoons honey (or a dash of stevia extract)
- 1 tablespoon maple syrup
- ½ tablespoon dry mustard
- ½ teaspoon ground ginger
- ½ teaspoon garlic powder
- Brown Rice for serving
- 1 tablespoon cornstarch + 1 tablespoon water

DIRECTIONS:

1. Place cubed chicken in bottom of crock (I use a 4 quart).
2. In bowl, combine soy sauce, honey/stevia, mustard, syrup, ginger, and garlic.
3. Pour mixture over chicken.
4. Cover and cook on low 6-8 hours.
5. Combine cornstarch and water. Stir into juices. Cover and let thicken.
6. Serve mixture over rice.

Yield: 4-5 servings

Notes:
- You don't need to thicken the juices if you don't want too – pour the juice over the rice and serve it all in a bowl. Then lap it up like a dog. I ain't proud.
- If you don't care for much salt, then use less-sodium soy sauce.
- My candida people can use sugar-free syrup.

This delicious recipe packs lots of flavor and a home-style Chinese take-out feel without all the MSG & other additives typical of some restaurant fare. It also doubled quite easily, leaving plenty of leftovers even after feeding our ravenous family of six.
++Scott: A Morefield Life

Main Dishes

Side Dishes

Hot Broccoli Salad

This recipe was born because I needed another veggie for this book and I wanted broccoli salad. So, I said to myself "Self, can you eat hot broccoli salad?" Self wasn't sure, so we tried. It turned out pretty stinkin' awesome. The answer is YES. And self is happy.

INGREDIENTS:

- 1½ pounds fresh broccoli florets
- ½ cup chopped red onion
- ¼ cup water
- 1 teaspoon salt
- ½ teaspoon minced garlic
- ¼ teaspoon pepper
- ¼ cup mayonnaise
- ¼ cup sour cream
- 1 teaspoon Apple Cider Vinegar
- 1 teaspoon Truvia (*I use homemade*) or 1 tablespoon sugar
- 2 tablespoons unsweetened, dried cranberries or goji berries
- 3 tablespoons chopped, cooked bacon

DIRECTIONS:

1. Combine broccoli, onion, water, salt, garlic, and pepper in a crock (4 quart).
2. Cover and cook on HIGH for 1½ hours. Drain.
3. In a small bowl, combine mayo, sour cream, ACV, and Truvia.
4. Stir mayo mixture into broccoli. Toss to coat.
5. Stir in bacon and cranberries.
6. Serve hot.

Yield: 5 servings

Notes:
- You know, if you don't want Hot Broccoli Salad, you can just mix everything all together with raw broccoli and call it Cold Broccoli Salad. This recipe is genius like that.
- I love the taste of goji berries in this instead of cranberries. I find mine at the local Amish store. Amish people rock.

While one would expect a heavy casserole, this dish is wonderfully light and allows the supporting flavors to add a subtle enhancement to a broccoli that is almost roasted in flavor, not soggy or limp. The leftovers are so good I ate them for breakfast the next day.
++Kimi: *See the Blue Sky*

Side Dishes

Crazy Easy Cabbage

I used to think I hated cabbage – I hated how it smelled and looked. It made me shiver and have nightmares...then something happened. I had it roasted. My life changed forever. Now, I look for all the many different ways to use it and I fight people at the Farmer's Market to get the best head – get outta my way, PAL! There is CABBAGE at this booth. *Shove*

INGREDIENTS:

- 1 head cabbage
- 1 teaspoon salt
- ½ teaspoon pepper (or less if you don't like pepper)
- 1 tablespoon butter
- 2 tablespoons soy sauce or Bragg's Liquid Aminos

DIRECTIONS:

1. Core and chop cabbage, not too small.
2. Place in crock (5-6 quart).
3. Sprinkle top with salt and pepper.
4. Cut butter into cubes and place on top.
5. Pour in soy sauce/Bragg's.
6. Cover and cook on high for one hour.
7. Stir and cook another hour on high.
8. Stir and serve (unless you need to cook longer based on desired tenderness).

Yield: 6 servings

Notes:
- If you cut your cabbage too small, it will just wither away to nothingness. I quarter mine, then slice thinly.
- Your crock will be FULL. And you'll think "WHOA!" But really, it cooks down. Don't freak out.

The title of this recipe pretty much sums it up for me. The only thing I would like to add is it's crazy delicious! When something is this crazy easy and this crazy delicious, it earns a permanent spot on my menu rotation.

++Mindy: Creating Naturally

Side Dishes

German Potato Salad

Confession – I don't really like potato salad. Seems kinda weird that I would include a recipe for it in MY cookbook. However, I married a man who likes it, so I indulge him sometimes. I won't tell you I liked this one...I did eat it. But it didn't really float my boat. If you don't like potato salad, you won't like this either. If you do like potato salad, this might just rock your world. The end.

INGREDIENTS:

- 2 pounds small red potatoes, halved
- 1 large onion, sliced into rings
- ¼ cup water
- 1½ tablespoons Apple Cider Vinegar
- 2 teaspoons Truvia (I use _homemade_) or 2 tablespoons sugar/xylitol/sucanat
- 1 teaspoon celery salt
- ½ teaspoon pepper
- ½ teaspoon dried mustard powder
- 1 tablespoon arrowroot + 1 tablespoon water
- ¼ cup chopped, cooked bacon

DIRECTIONS:

1. Combine potatoes, onion, water, ACV, sweetener, celery salt, pepper, and mustard in a crock (5 quart).
2. Cover and cook on low for 8 hours.
3. In a small bowl, combine arrowroot and water.
4. Stir arrowroot mixture into potatoes along with bacon. Stir well. Let stand until thickened.

Yield: 5 servings

Notes:
- This potato salad is meant to be eaten warm...but cold is cool too. Get it?
- Cornstarch is acceptable if you don't use arrowroot, or you can use ½ teaspoon glucomannan.
- If you are low-carb, consider using radishes instead of potatoes.

This was a super easy throwback to a warm and filling comfort food! Very tasty with pork chops.
++Sara: Your Thriving Family

Sweet Bacon Green Beans

Green Beans are one of my favorite veggies. Bacon is one of my favorite foods – it only makes sense to combine the two. I added a dash of stevia to give them a slightly sweet/salty taste...kinda like Kettle Corn, but without the corn or popping – so really not like Kettle Corn at all. Sorry, I'm hungry and want Kettle Corn... send reinforcements.

© 2013 Stacy Myers | Keep Crockin' | Stacy Makes Cents

INGREDIENTS:

- 4 cups frozen green beans
- ½ cup chicken stock/broth
- 8 pieces cooked bacon, chopped
- Dash stevia
- ½ teaspoon salt
- ¼ teaspoon pepper
- ¼ teaspoon onion powder
- ¼ teaspoon garlic powder

DIRECTIONS:

1. Combine all in small crock (2-4 quart).
2. Cover and cook on high for 2 hours.
3. Serve with slotted spoon.

Yield: 4 servings

Notes:
- You can leave the sweetener out...I was just embracing my Southern heritage. Barry doesn't like them sweet...but he doesn't like cottage cheese either. Weirdo.
- This recipe easily doubles or triples based on how much you need.

Bacon - check. Green Beans - check. The goodness that is this super simple is unbelievable! We tried them with and without stevia. I preferred without; my hubby and toddler loved the stevia version. This will be a side at our holiday tables for sure!!!
++Allison: The Life of a Novice

Side Dishes

Creamed Peas

Not gonna lie. The name, Creamed Peas sounds like something I should be feeding my baby. It kinda makes me smush my nose up funny. Uhhhh, no thanks. But, if you do turn your nose up at these, it will be a sad, sad day. Because even though the name is weird, the taste is AWESOME. They. Are. Good. Go ahead and feed them to your baby – if you feel like sharing… which I usually don't.

INGREDIENTS:

- 12 ounces frozen peas
- 2 ounces cream cheese, cubed
- 1 teaspoon salt
- ½ teaspoon onion powder
- ¼ teaspoon pepper

DIRECTIONS:

1. Place peas in a greased crock (2 quart).
2. Sprinkle with salt, onion powder, and pepper.
3. Place cream cheese on top.
4. Cover and cook on high for 2 hours.
5. Stir and serve.

Yield: 3 servings

Notes:
- This recipe is easily doubled or tripled. It would make an excellent Thanksgiving side dish!
- There is no added water for this recipe because the frozen peas make enough moisture.

This dish disappeared in one sitting! My two year olds scarfed them down without even waiting for them to cool off – definitely on the menu again for next week!
++Jennifer: Growing Up Triplets

Side Dishes

Squash Casserole

This might be one of my favorite side dishes of all time — for real. I used to make it in the oven...but now I've figured out how to make it in the crock... because I rock like that. Rock, crock. Rock, crock. That rhymes!

© 2013 Stacy Myers | Keep Crockin' | Stacy Makes Cents

INGREDIENTS:

- 4 medium summer squash, sliced
- ½ cup chopped onion
- 2 eggs
- ¼ cup mayonnaise
- ¼ cup sour cream
- ½ cup shredded cheddar
- 1 teaspoon salt
- ¼ teaspoon pepper
- 2 tablespoons Parmesan cheese

DIRECTIONS:

1. Lay squash in the bottom of a greased crock (4-5 quart).
2. Sprinkle onion over top.
3. In a small bowl, combine eggs, mayo, sour cream, cheddar, salt and pepper.
4. Pour evenly over squash and spread.
5. Sprinkle top with Parmesan.
6. Cover and cook on HIGH for 1½-2 hours or until set in the middle.
7. Let stand 15 minutes before serving.

Yield: 4 servings

Notes:
- This should also work with zucchini...but I have never tried it. Because I like this with squash — and I like routine and structure in my life.
- Any type of shredded cheese would work — but cheddar is best. On second thought, only use cheddar.

"Get in my belly!" ++Stacy-ism

Side Dishes

Loaded Broccoli & Cauliflower

Who needs potatoes? They make my butt jiggle. Give me broccoli and cauliflower instead! Yes, they cause other "issues," but at least they are issues without excess rear baggage. And I promise, after making this dish you won't miss them. Cauli is the new potato (I heard that on Pinterest.)

INGREDIENTS:

- 1 head cauliflower, steamed or roasted OR 1 (12 ounce) bag frozen cauliflower and 1 (12 ounce) bag frozen broccoli
- 4 tablespoons butter, melted
- 1 cup sour cream
- 1 tablespoon dried minced onion
- ½ tablespoon dried parsley
- 1 teaspoon salt
- ½ teaspoon garlic powder
- ¼ teaspoon pepper
- 8 sliced bacon, cooked and chopped
- 1 cup shredded cheddar cheese

DIRECTIONS:

1. Place cooked cauli and broccoli in the bottom of a greased crock (5 quart).
2. Combine butter, sour cream, minced onion, parsley, salt, garlic powder, pepper, and ½ cup shredded cheddar.
3. Spoon sour cream mixture over veggies.
4. Sprinkle with remaining cheese and bacon pieces.
5. Cover and cook on HIGH 1½ hours.

Yield: 5 servings

Notes:
- This also doubles well and a 5 quart is still big enough. You might want to cook 2 hours.
- Other types of cheese are acceptable...I'm just a creature of habit and cheddar is my fave.

This was a hit at our small group dinner. My husband said to put it on the regular rotation, and even our picky eater and kids loved it!
++Mary Beth: New Life Steward

Side Dishes

Tomato Crisp

My mama makes something similar to this dish and she calls it Baked Tomatoes. It's sweet and this is savory. Barry doesn't like Baked Tomatoes (he's weird, but I still love him) but he enjoys this savory version – I'm not sure he can be trusted since he doesn't like plain cottage cheese.

INGREDIENTS:

- 2 (14.5 ounce) cans diced tomatoes, drained (or 2½ cups diced fresh tomatoes)
- ½ cup fresh breadcrumbs
- 2 tablespoons Parmesan cheese
- Salt and pepper to taste
- ¼ teaspoon garlic powder
- ¼ teaspoon onion powder
- ¼ teaspoon oregano

DIRECTIONS:

1. Place drained tomatoes in bottom of a small crock (2 quart).
2. Combine breadcrumbs, cheese, salt and pepper, garlic powder, onion powder, and oregano.
3. Sprinkle breadcrumb mixture over tomatoes.
4. Cover and cook on HIGH for 2 hours. Serve hot.

Yield: 4 servings

Notes:
- This recipe is easily doubled, however you don't need to double the size of the crock
- If you use fresh tomatoes, make sure to seed them first.

There is so much depth of flavor in this easy side dish. It's comfort food – Italian style!
++Justyn: Creative Christian Mama

Side Dishes

Zucchini Bake

Zucchini is one of those veggies that grows in abundance in the summer and fall — if you have a green thumb, that is. If you're like me, you're glad other people have a green thumb...because mine is the BLACK THUMB OF DEATH.

INGREDIENTS:

- 4 cups shredded zucchini
- 1 cup almond flour or ¾ cup white wheat flour
- ½ teaspoon baking powder
- ½ teaspoon salt
- ½ teaspoon onion powder
- ¼ teaspoon pepper
- ¼ teaspoon oregano
- ½ cup shredded cheddar cheese
- 2 eggs
- ¼ cup Greek yogurt or sour cream

DIRECTIONS:

1. Combine all ingredients.
2. Pour into greased crock (4-5 quart).
3. Cover and cook on HIGH for 1½-2 hours or until knife inserted in center comes out clean.

Yield: 5 servings

Notes:
- Summer squash would also be a good option in this dish.
- If you LOVE cheese, go ahead and sprinkle more on top. I won't tell.

The instructions were clear and easy to follow. Tastes super! I used almond flour and it worked out great as a side dish. I need to make some more because my husband ate all the leftovers. ++Marianne: Ragdoll Kitchen

Side Dishes

Cumin Carrots

Okay, don't run away. I realize this sounds weird. I mean, don't normal people eat their carrots candied with sugar and cinnamon? Well...I ain't normal. And I love cumin. So, I try to work it in whenever I can. Give these a try – you'll like them. And if you don't, feed 'em to the dog... waste not, want not. That totally fits here, right?

INGREDIENTS:

- 1 pound baby carrots or whole carrots, peeled and cut into slices
- 1 tablespoon butter
- 2 teaspoons cumin
- ½ teaspoon salt
- Dash pepper

DIRECTIONS:

1. Combine all ingredients in a small crock – I use my 2 quart for one pound of carrots.
2. Cover and cook on HIGH for 1 hour.
3. Stir.
4. Cover and cook another 1-1½ hours or until carrots are tender.
5. Stir and serve.

Yield: 4 servings

Notes:
- This recipe can easily be doubled or tripled. You will just need to use a larger crock.
- Hate cumin? We can still be friends. Use cinnamon instead...but don't call them Cumin Carrots. Then they'll be Cinnamon Carrots.

I loved the cumin carrots, they're a subtle twist on basic steamed carrots that will be added to my recipe repertoire. I made carrot coins and doubled the recipe for my 5 qt crock. ++Kate: Venison for Dinner

Side Dishes

Desserts

Maple Pecan Pie

You want to know how to make a man happy? I'll tell you. Make him this pie. Of course, it also works for mothers and children. And wives. And random people who stop by to visit. I love making men happy. And I love stuffing my face with a pie that I said I made for him - pie, the gift you can give to yourself...and a man.

INGREDIENTS:

- 1 cup almond flour
- ¼ cup sugar/xylitol/sucanat
- 3 tablespoons melted coconut oil
- 1 teaspoon vanilla
- 1 cup sugar/xylitol/sucanat
- 3 eggs, beaten
- ¼ cup maple syrup (or sugar free syrup for my candida friends)
- 1 stick butter, melted (½ cup)
- 1 teaspoon vanilla
- 1 teaspoon maple extract
- 1 cup chopped pecans

DIRECTIONS:

1. Combine almond flour, ¼ cup sugar, melted coconut oil and 1 teaspoon vanilla.
2. Place in bottom of a greased crock (5 quart) and press down evenly.
3. Combine 1 cup sugar through pecans. Mix well.
4. Spread filling evenly over crust.
5. Cover and cook on high for 2 hours or until set.
6. Let stand 1 hour before serving – so the filling can fully set up.

Yield: 6-8 servings

Notes:
- Butter will pool around the edges. Try to avoid sucking it up through a straw. BHAHAHAHA! Okay, I'm totally kidding, go ahead and drink it. Yummorama.
- Upon standing, the butter will absorb back into the pie.
- Serve warm with vanilla ice cream and get proposed to all over again.

Not only was this recipe amazingly quick to put together, but it stands out as the most amazing pecan pie I have ever tasted! My family, who is not as easy to please as I am, agree wholeheartedly! Stacy totally rocked the house with this recipe. Our family of 6 gives this 12 thumbs up!   ++Amanda: Counting All Joy

Desserts

Fruit Enchiladas

Okay, so I'll admit. These aren't much to look at. Only a mother could love them – but dude, take one bite and you won't care if they look like a dirty sock; you'd eat them anyway.

© 2013 Stacy Myers | Keep Crockin' | Stacy Makes Cents

INGREDIENTS:

- 3 cups frozen or fresh berries
- ¼ cup sugar/xylitol/sucanat or ⅛ teaspoon stevia extract
- 1 stick butter (½ cup)
- ½ cup sugar/xylitol/sucanat
- 1 teaspoon vanilla
- ½ cup water
- 6 tortillas
- 2 tablespoons sugar/sucanat/xylitol
- 1 teaspoon cinnamon
- Ice Cream for serving

DIRECTIONS:

1. Toss berries with ¼ cup sugar.
2. Divide berry mixture between the 6 tortillas. Roll up.
3. Place tortillas in the bottom of a crock (5 quart). It's okay to squish them to fit.
4. In a small saucepan, heat butter, ½ cup sugar, vanilla, and water until butter is melted and sugar is dissolved. Do not boil.
5. Pour sugar syrup over tortillas.
6. Combine 3 tablespoons sugar and cinnamon. Sprinkle over all.
7. Cover and cook on high 2 hours.
8. Let stand 30 minutes before serving. Serve hot with ice cream.
9. Serve with slotted spoon.

Yield: 3-6 servings

Notes:
- Hate berries (lame)? Use other fruit like peaches or plums.
- There will be juice in the bottom of the crock. Save it and reheat in the morning for a great pancake/waffle topping!

I was honestly skeptical about this recipe, but it was so easy to make and delicious! Everyone in my family loved it, even my pickiest girl asked for seconds. We enjoyed it with homemade coconut ice cream.

++Marilyn: Just Making Noise

Desserts

Crustless Pumpkin "Pie"

Pie is in quotes because this dish is more like a baked squash side-dish – the consistency isn't as firm as a pumpkin pie and there isn't any crust. But hey, I needed another dessert to make this an even 10. So, PIE it is...and we sure didn't struggle to down it for dessert.

INGREDIENTS:

- 1 (15 ounce) can pumpkin (NOT pie mix) or 1¾ cups pumpkin puree
- 1½ cups almond milk (or regular milk)
- ½ teaspoon stevia extract or ¾ cup sugar
- 3 tablespoons coconut flour
- 2 eggs
- 2 tablespoons melted butter
- 1 teaspoon vanilla extract
- 1 teaspoon cinnamon
- ½ teaspoon nutmeg
- ½ teaspoon ginger
- ¼ teaspoon ground cloves
- Whipped cream for serving

DIRECTIONS:

1. Combine all ingredients (except whipped cream) and whisk well to combine.
2. Pour into greased crock (5 quart).
3. Cover and cook on high for about 2 hours or until set.
4. Let stand 30 minutes before serving.

Yield: 6 servings

Notes:
- Try this with pureed butternut squash instead of pumpkin.
- Melted coconut oil could be substituted for the butter.

This Pumpkin "Pie" couldn't be easier. I even whisked the ingredients together right in the crock pot because I had just cleaned the kitchen and didn't want to dirty another dish. I love that when you use stevia this dessert is healthy enough to enjoy for breakfast, or even as a side dish!
++Anne: Authentic Simplicity

Desserts

Stuffed Apples

You won't feel stuffed after you eat these lovely apples – unlike on Thanksgiving when you eat more turkey than you weigh and you cover it in 2 gallons of gravy and then you eat two pieces of pie with ice cream…and then you have a detox bath the next day.

INGREDIENTS:

- 6 apples (I like Roman or Stayman)
- ½ cup brown sugar/xylitol/sucanat
- ½ cup granola of choice (I like using grain free granola)
- 1 teaspoon cinnamon
- ½ teaspoon nutmeg
- 2 tablespoons melted butter
- 1 teaspoon vanilla extract
- ¼ cup lemon juice
- ¼ cup water
- 10 drops liquid stevia extract
- Vanilla ice cream

DIRECTIONS:

1. Core apples, leaving bottoms intact so filling won't fall out.
2. Place apples in bottom of crock (depending on size of apples, crock size will vary).
3. In a mixing bowl, combine sugar, granola, cinnamon, nutmeg, butter and vanilla.
4. Fill apple centers with granola mixture.
5. Combine lemon juice, water, and liquid stevia. Pour into bottom of crock but not over top of apples.
6. Cover and cook on high 2-3 hours or until apples are tender to your liking.
7. Serve with ice cream.

Yield: 6 servings

Notes:

- This recipe halves easily…and it probably doubles well too, but I've never seen a crock that big. You'd have to bake them in the oven.
- Save the juice found in the bottom of the crock for serving over pancakes. BUTTER!!!!!

Being a busy mom of two small children, I'm always looking for recipes that are easy and nourishing - recipes my whole family will love. These "baked" apples meet the criteria perfectly. Not only are they delicious and healthy, but they are easy to make and enjoyed by our whole family.
++Kristin: Live Simply

Desserts

Cocoa Peanut Butter Fondue

Fondue is such a fun word to say. Fondue. Fondue. Fooonnnndddduuee. Plus, it just makes me feel fancy. Fondue is really just a formal way to say: hot runny dip. But doesn't Fondue sound so much better than Hot Runny Dip?

INGREDIENTS:

- ½ cup natural peanut butter
- ¼ cup cocoa powder
- ⅓ cup sugar/xylitol/sucanat
- ½ cup heavy cream
- 1 teaspoon vanilla
- Additional cream or milk to thin

DIRECTIONS:

1. Combine all in a small bowl. Whisk well to combine.
2. Pour into small crock (2 quart).
3. Cover and cook on high for 1 hour. Stir. Add milk to thin to desired consistency.
4. Turn to "warm" setting to use as fondue.

Yield: about 1⅓ cups fondue

Notes:
- You may want to add more sugar or some additional stevia if you desire a very sweet fondue.
- Almond butter could also be used in place of the peanut butter.
- Serve with fruit or cookies. Shortbread would be excellent!
- Store in fridge (if there is any left) and reheat as needed.

I have a heart for French culture, especially cuisine, so fondue was an obvious choice! This was so easy to put together, leave, and come back to finished and ready to eat and let me tell you- you will eat every last drop! This will be a go-to dessert for us from this point on!   ++Erinn: Embracing Everything

Desserts

Cinnamon Chip Mason Jar Cheesecake

So, I saw this idea for Mason jar cheesecakes on Pinterest. Of course, I knew I would make a healthy version in the crock...because I try to make everything in the crock. It's a disease I have. There is no cure – but eating cheesecake helps.

INGREDIENTS:

- 1 cup almond flour
- ¼ cup sugar/xylitol/sucanat
- 3 tablespoons melted butter
- 1 teaspoon vanilla
- 1 (8 ounce) cream cheese, softened
- ½ cup cottage cheese
- ½ cup sugar/xylitol/sucanat
- 2 eggs
- 2 teaspoons vanilla
- 1 teaspoon cinnamon
- 6 teaspoons mini chocolate chips

DIRECTIONS:

1. Combine almond flour, ¼ cup sugar, melted butter and vanilla.
2. Divide evenly between 6, 8 ounce GREASED mason jars. Press crust down lightly.
3. In food processor, combine cream cheese, cottage cheese, ½ cup sugar, eggs, vanilla, and cinnamon. Process until smooth.
4. Divide filling between jars.
5. Sprinkle each jar with 1 teaspoon of mini chocolate chips.
6. Place jars down in large crock (my 5 quart works great). Only one layer.
7. Pour about ½ inch of water in the both of the crock to create a water bath.
8. Cover top with tea towel (to catch condensation) and place lid on crock.
9. Cook on high for 1½ hours.
10. Remove jars and let cool completely at room temperature.
11. Refrigerate overnight.

Yield: 6 servings

Notes:
- You may use coconut oil in place of the butter for the crust.
- Use this as a base recipe for your favorite cheesecake recipes: omit cinnamon and chips and add fruit for a berry cheesecake. Or sprinkle the top with nuts and use your favorite extract.
- Refrigerating overnight always yields the best cheesecake result. I know it's hard to wait. Pretend it will make you get sick unless you let it sit overnight. That will work.

What a great recipe! My youngest son always chooses cheesecake for a dessert or birthday treat. He loved this recipe and so do I. This was simple, delicious and healthy, plus it is cute!! This is a new favorite in our home and will be made often!!
++Mary: The Encouraging Home

Desserts

Almond Flour Brownies

This is a take on my _Almond Flour Brownies_ for the oven. I only changed it up a bit with the addition of the chocolate chips. I tried to tell myself it was really for my 4 year old. But who am I kidding? I don't care how old you are, chocolate chips are kickin' awesome. So are brownies. Making these in the crock gives them extra crunchy edges. My favorite! Forget the 4 year old. These are MINE.

INGREDIENTS:

- 2 ounces unsweetened baking chocolate
- ½ cup butter (one stick)
- ½ cup sugar/xylitol/sucanat
- ¼ teaspoon stevia extract (I use NuNaturals)
- 2 eggs
- 1 teaspoon vanilla
- Dash salt
- ¼ teaspoon baking soda
- ½ cup almond flour
- ¼ cup chocolate chips
- ¼ cup chopped nuts

DIRECTIONS:

1. In a small saucepan, melt chocolate and butter. Cool slightly.
2. Stir in sugar, stevia, eggs, vanilla, salt, baking soda, and almond flour.
3. Fold in chocolate chips and nuts.
4. Pour into well greased crock (5 quart).
5. Cover and cook on high 1½-2 hours or until done in center.
6. Cool before cutting.

Yield: 8 brownies

Notes:
- I love these with chopped cashews.
- You'll get a slightly crispy outside edge with this recipe – which is always awesome. Gooey in the middle and crunchy on the edges. Who could ask for anything more? Do NOT overcrock.

Moist, delicious and gobbled up in no time. My family loved these and I love having the option of making brownies in the crockpot. Highly recommend you make these today! ++Karen: _The Fruit of Her Hands_

Desserts

Peanut Butter Lava "Cake"

I should call this Peanut Butter Lava Crack. Because after one bite, you'll be addicted. Then again, one does not really want to associate peanut butter with the word "crack." It's not a word that conjures up happiness. More like "I need to poke my eyeballs out." But yeah – this is yummy stuff.

INGREDIENTS:

- 1 cup almond flour
- ½ cup sugar/xylitol/sucanat
- 2 teaspoons baking powder
- ½ teaspoon salt
- 1 tablespoon coconut oil
- ½ cup peanut butter (no sugar added)
- ¾ cup milk (whole or almond)
- 2 teaspoons vanilla extract
- ¼ cup peanut flour (you can use PB2)
- ¼ cup sugar/xylitol/sucanat
- 1 cup boiling water
- Ice Cream for serving

DIRECTIONS:

1. Combine flour, ½ cup sugar, baking powder, and salt in a mixing bowl.
2. In a saucepan, melt peanut butter and coconut oil, just until smooth. Remove from heat.
3. Stir in milk and vanilla.
4. Combine liquid and flour ingredients. Whisk well.
5. Pour into greased crock (4 quart).
6. In a small bowl, combine peanut flour and ¼ cup sugar. Whisk well to break up clumps.
7. Sprinkle over batter.
8. Pour boiling water over all. DO NOT STIR.
9. Cover and cook on high for 2 hours or until edges are set. (Center will remain jiggly.)
10. Let stand about 30 minutes before serving.
11. Serve warm with ice cream.

Yield: 5-6 servings

Notes:
- Because I use almond flour in this cake, it's not the normal "Lava Cake" consistency. It's only set around the edges and full of pudding in the center. Only cook until the edges are set when you press them with your finger.
- If you wanted to try all purpose flour in lieu of almond flour, you might get a more Lava Cake-like cake. I have not tried it, so proceed at your own risk. However, note that there are NO eggs in this cake...so, no matter what, if it didn't work you could still eat it in the closet alone with a spoon.

This wonderfully creamy cake has a soft, rich, pudding-like consistency and did not disappoint! We served it while still warm with a little ice cream, and the pickiest little eater at my table had extras.

++Melanie: Treasures Unseen

Desserts

Coconut Chocolate Spoon Cake

Sometimes I concoct a recipe and it doesn't quite work out – the first time I made this one, it was so wet and watery it looked like I left it in the rain. So, it took some tweaking, which just means more chocolate eating for me. And well, sometimes research is just a heavy burden to bear. *Sigh*

INGREDIENTS:

- ⅓ cup coconut flour
- ¼ cup sugar/xylitol/sucanat
- 3 tablespoons cocoa powder
- 1 teaspoon baking powder
- Dash salt
- 3 tablespoons melted virgin coconut oil
- 1 egg
- ⅓ cup almond milk
- 1 teaspoon vanilla extract
- 3 tablespoons sugar/xylitol/sucanat
- 1 tablespoon cocoa powder
- ½ cup boiling water

DIRECTIONS:

1. Grease a 2-4 quart crock (I like my 2 quart best for this dessert).
2. In a mixing bowl, combine coconut flour, sugar, cocoa, baking powder, salt, coconut oil, egg, almond milk, and vanilla. Whisk well to combine.
3. Pour into crock and smooth evenly.
4. In a small bowl, combine 3 tablespoons sugar with 1 tablespoon cocoa.
5. Sprinkle mixture over top of batter.
6. Pour boiling water evenly over all. DO NOT STIR.
7. Cover and cook on high for 2 hours or until toothpick inserted in center comes out clean.
8. Let stand 30 minutes before serving.

Yield: 4-5 servings

Notes:
- This is a very moist (I hate that word) "cake." It will almost be hard to scoop out...and then it will melt in your mouth. I'm hungry...is anyone else hungry?
- No, I have not tried this with anything except coconut flour. I don't know the ratio for substitutions – substitute at your own risk...and realize there might be ruined chocolate at stake.
- This is best HOT and fresh...and not as good left over. However, I never struggled to eat the leftovers. *Burp*

This deeelicious cake was chocolatey, gooey goodness that the whole family loved. It was sweet, tasty, and - dare I say it - moist. Don't tell, but I snuck my toddler's portion when she wasn't looking. Shhh.

++Christy: The Simple Homemaker

Desserts

Apple Cinnamon Coffee Cake

I was unsure if I should put this in the dessert section or the breakfast section. Isn't that a lovely problem to have? Hmmmmm. I'm not sure if I should have cake for dessert or cake for breakfast. Maybe both. Yes, both. Good decision.

INGREDIENTS:

- 2 medium apples, peeled, cored, and chopped
- 3 tablespoons sugar/xylitol/sucanat
- 2 teaspoons cinnamon
- ½ cup coconut flour
- ½ cup sugar/xylitol/sucanat
- 2 teaspoons baking powder
- Dash salt
- 4 eggs
- 1 cup milk (whole or almond)
- ¼ cup melted butter or coconut oil
- 2 teaspoons vanilla extract
- 2 tablespoons sugar/xylitol/sucanant
- 1 teaspoon cinnamon

DIRECTIONS:

1. Combine chopped apples, 3 tablespoons sugar, and 2 teaspoons cinnamon. Toss to coat.
2. Place apple mixture in the bottom of a greased crock pot (5 quart).
3. In a mixing bowl, combine coconut flour, ½ cup sugar, baking powder, salt, eggs, milk, butter and vanilla. Whisk well to combine.
4. Pour batter over apples and spread evenly.
5. Combine 2 tablespoons sugar and 1 teaspoon cinnamon. Sprinkle evenly over batter.
6. Cover and cook on high for 2 hours or until toothpick comes out clean when inserted in center.
7. Let stand 20 minutes before serving. Serve hot with whipped cream or ice cream.

Yield: 6 servings

Notes:
- This is a very moist cake due to the coconut flour and egg combo. It's only slightly sweet, not one of the types of coffee cakes that puts you into a sugar coma.
- Pears would also work great! But then it would be PEAR Cinnamon Coffee Cake.
- You don't have to peel your apples. We like the extra fiber boost. Regularity is under-rated.

I am a recipe tweaker by nature, but honestly this recipe came out so perfectly I don't care change a thing. WOW! The flavor was magical, and the amount of sweetener was absolutely perfect – no sick sugar bellies!
++Lea: Nourishing Treasures

Desserts

About the Author - Meet Stacy

Stacy is the author of _Crock On: A Semi-Whole Foods Slow Cooker Cookbook_ and a stay-at-home and homeschooling mom to her two children, Annie (June 2009) and Andy (August 2012). After an "awakening" in March 2011, she and her family switched to a more natural, whole foods diet.

Stacy likes to blog about how to live on less than you make and how to eat good food while doing it. Her passion is teaching others how to save money and she tag teams with her husband in this endeavor.

On her blog, _Stacy Makes Cents_, you'll find information on how to save money in the kitchen, how to have fun with your kids, and how to be thrifty in all areas of life.

Make sure to follow her on Facebook, Twitter, Instagram and more to keep up with her daily antics.

 facebook.com/stacymakescents

 twitter.com/stacymakescents

 pinterest.com/stacymakescents

 instagram.com/stacymakescents

 stacymakescents.com/rss

 youtube.com/stacymakescents

Made in the USA
Charleston, SC
26 November 2013